What in the World Is a Drum?

Mary Elizabeth Salzmann

Consulting Editor, Diane Craig, M.A./Reading Specialist

A Division of ABDO

ABDO
Publishing Company

visit us at www.abdopublishing.com

Published by ABDO Publishing Company, a division of ABDO, P.O. Box 398166, Minneapolis, Minnesota 55439. Copyright © 2012 by Abdo Consulting Group, Inc. International copyrights reserved in all countries. No part of this book may be reproduced in any form without written permission from the publisher. Super SandCastle™ is a trademark and logo of ABDO Publishing Company.

Printed in the United States of America, North Mankato, Minnesota
092011
012012

 PRINTED ON RECYCLED PAPER

Editor: Elissa Mann
Content Developer: Nancy Tuminelly
Cover and Interior Design: Colleen Dolphin, Mighty Media, Inc.
Interior Production: Kelsey Gullickson
Photo Credits: Shutterstock, Thinkstock

Library of Congress Cataloging-in-Publication Data

Salzmann, Mary Elizabeth, 1968-

 What in the world is a drum? / Mary Elizabeth Salzmann.

   p. cm. -- (Musical instruments)

 ISBN 978-1-61783-204-8

 1. Drum--Juvenile literature. I. Title.

 ML1035.S25 2012

 786.9'19--dc23

                          2011023173

Super SandCastle™ books are created by a team of professional educators, reading specialists, and content developers around five essential components— phonemic awareness, phonics, vocabulary, text comprehension, and fluency—to assist young readers as they develop reading skills and strategies and increase their general knowledge. All books are written, reviewed, and leveled for guided reading, early reading intervention, and Accelerated Reader® programs for use in shared, guided, and independent reading and writing activities to support a balanced approach to literacy instruction.

Contents

What Is a

A drum is a musical instrument.

Drum?

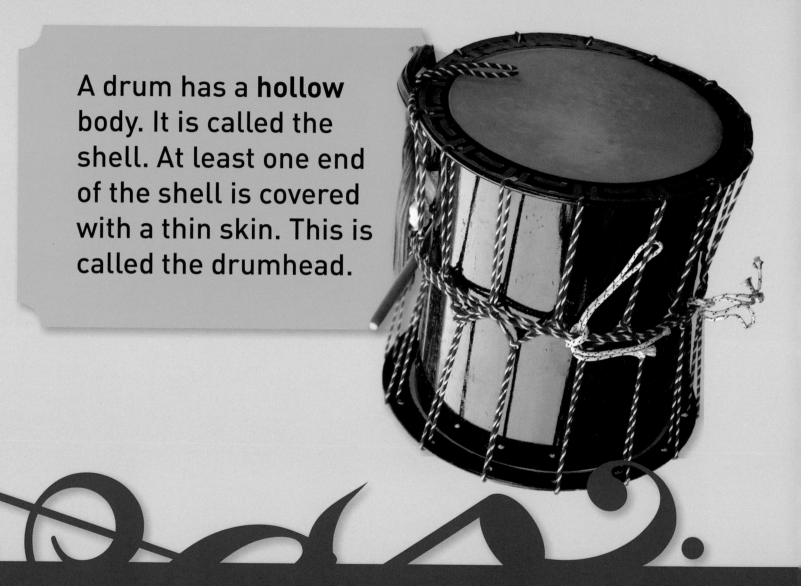

A drum has a **hollow** body. It is called the shell. At least one end of the shell is covered with a thin skin. This is called the drumhead.

drumhead

shell

There are many different kinds of drums. Most drums have round drumheads. The shell of a drum can be almost any shape.

To play the drum, the drummer hits the drumhead. Some drums are hit with the hands.

Some drums are hit with drumsticks.

Let's Play

the Drum!

Robert is in the school marching band. He plays a huge **bass** drum.

Katelyn is playing a drum set. It has a tom-tom drum, a snare drum, and a **bass** drum. It also has a **cymbal**.

tom-tom

cymbal

snare

bass

Seth is playing a conga drum. His dad is playing the bongos.

Maria likes to play the **djembe**.
Once a week she plays in a **drum
circle** with other drummers.

Find the Drum

a.   b.   c.   d.

d. violin   **c.** flute   **b.** drum (correct)   **a.** clarinet

Drum Quiz

1. Drums have a **hollow** body. True or False?

2. There is only one kind of drum. True or False?

3. Drums are never played with the hands. True or False?

4. Robert plays a **bass** drum. True or False?

5. Maria plays in a **drum circle** once a week. True or False?

ANSWERS: **1.** true **2.** false **3.** false **4.** true **5.** true

Glossary

bass – a type of voice or musical instrument that makes the lowest sound. It is pronounced with a long a sound, like base.

cymbal – an instrument shaped like a plate. A cymbal can be hit with drumsticks, or two cymbals can be banged together.

djembe – a kind of drum from Africa. It is pronounced *JEM-bay*.

drum circle – a group of people that sit in a circle and play hand drums together.

hollow – having an empty space inside.